Table of Contents

Page

(continued)

Robert W. Pike, CSP

So why would we publish a book of magic tricks for trainers?

The answer is simple. I believe in instructor-led, participant-centered training. This is the foundation concept of Creative Training Techniques® and magic can be a part of that. Magic captures the attention, fires up the imagination, and involves people. Have you ever said, "How did s/he do that?"

But the magic is the medium, the application and the learning point that comes along with it is the real message. And that's the real reason for this book — to give you the medium and let you supply the message or application.

For example, I use the magic coloring book in a number of seminars. The concept of the coloring book is simple: At first the pages are all blank, next they have outlines as any coloring book would have, then the outlines are fully colored, and finally the pages are all blank. The audience is astonished. The trick itself is fun, but it's the story that gives the application and that makes the point.

Let me illustrate. In Creative Training Techniques® I might close using the magic coloring book this way: Designing and delivering a training program is a lot like a coloring book for your children or a niece or nephew. You want the coloring book to be personal, so you don't buy it, you make it. You take a colorful cover and staple it to a bunch of blank pages (Here you hold up the coloring book, show the cover, and riffle the pages to show the blank pages.) Then you start to think about what subjects they would get excited about, that would really pique their interest — it might be planes or trains, cowboys or astronauts, mountains, oceans, the zoo, or the circus. When you decide on the topics you start tracing outlines on the blank pages (Riffle the pages to show the outlines.).

You do the same thing with a training program. You do a needs assessment to find out the skills and knowledge that would really pay off for the participants. You design the handouts, instructor materials, activities, and visual aids with that knowledge and those skills in mind. Yet at this point all we have is a training program — or a coloring book to color — neither means a thing until people are involved.

Now, there are three colors that computer monitors use to generate all the colors we see on a screen — red, green, and blue. I want you to get one of those colors in mind, imagine one of them in your fist, and when I count to three yell out your choice and at the same time throw the imaginary color from your fist to the coloring book. (I hold the coloring book up.) If you yell loud enough we only do this once. (Generally there's laughter.) Ready, one, two, three. (Everybody yells their color and throws it at the book.) I then riffle the pages and they see all the color. Then I say, "You see it takes your energy, participation, and enthusiasm to make the coloring book really come to life. And you know without your energy, enthusiasm, and participation we have nothing at all. (I riffle the pages to show that they are blank again.) So remember when it come to training you are the magic!

The story is important, because it is the story that helps apply the magic trick which they are involved in to some practical application — and the application is the key. In some cases in this book we supply you with an application. In other words it's up to you. In future editions of this book we would like to supply applications that have worked for you with the various tricks. So write to me, tell me how you've used it, along with the story that you've used. And maybe you'll see your story and name in the next edition!

How do I come up with stories? I start by practicing the trick without a story at all. My first goal is to master the steps so that I can perform the trick flawlessly without having to think about the steps. I also spend time practicing in front of the mirror or practicing with a video camera recording so that I can play it back and look at it from the audience's perspective. Along the way I start thinking about what each part of the trick might mean. I don't try to force it. I just think about it for a bit, then let my subconscious work on it. By the time I've mastered the trick, the story and application have taken shape.

Remember the story and application are as important as the trick. In training we use magic to make a point — not simply to have fun, entertain, etc!

Some tricks you'll master quite easily — others will take more time, but it won't be long before you have half a dozen tricks you can use in various places. Here are a few other guidelines:

1. Use the tricks sparingly and consider spacing them out. Don't let training get lost in the entertainment.

2. Never perform a trick more than once. Most tricks are so simple that if the audience gets into a mode of trying to figure every one out they won't be listening to your story or application at all!

3. Unless you are teaching an audience to do a trick, never reveal how it is done. The only reason for explaining how a trick is performed is to teach the person to perform it. No one appreciates having someone ruin a trick for an entire group by explaining it! Don't take away the wonder!

This book can be used in several ways:

1. You can choose to go through it from cover to cover — to familiarize yourself with everything that's available. Then go back and learn the tricks you feel have application.

2. You can start with tricks that you feel are easiest for you. That may be tricks with foolproof props like the magic coloring

book, or the boomerangs, or tricks that
require no props at all.

The most important thing to do, though, is to start somewhere. If at first a trick doesn't work the way you'd like,
set it aside and come back to it a little later. All of the
tricks in this book were designed to be as easy to master
as possible for enthusiastic amateurs! So get ready to
add a new dimension to your presentations — with
tricks for trainers — magic with a message!

This first section contains magic that requires special props. Most of them can be made from materials readily available or check with Resources for Organizations, Inc. for the availability of these props.

What's the Difference?

This routine utilizes two boomerangs produced with a reusable writing surface. It is particularly effective when used in comparing two components since either boomerang can be shown longer or shorter than the other one.....or both can be shown as being the same size!

Gone!

Anything wrapped up in this handkerchief disappears!

Uplifting!

A clear plastic glass is placed on a book and covered with a handkerchief. The littlest child in the audience is able to lift it from the book, but you can make it so that the strongest adult will not be able to lift it!

String Sensation

Two pieces of string are shown and placed in a spectator's hand. As you pull on the ends of the string, the spectator will feel the string actually join together in his hand!

Magic Message

Two slates are shown blank on both sides. They are placed face to face with a piece of chalk placed between them. When the slates are held up to the ear of a spectator, she can actually hear the chalk writing. When the slates are separated, a message of your choice appears on the slates!

Sawing a Person In Half

Two spectators help to tie ropes around the waist of a third audience member. As the ropes are pulled, the spectator can feel them tighten around her waist! Yet when the ropes are pulled quickly, they visibly melt right through the waist of the volunteer!

Hercules Outdone

Picking up two nails, you bend them in your bare hands!

Giant Three Card Monte

Three large cards are shown with the odd card in the middle of the spread. The cards are turned slowly over and still when the center card is removed, the card contains a special message for introducing the topic of the training!

Clipit

Five playing cards are glued together in an overlapping row to prove that no manipulation of the cards is possible. Nevertheless, when the cards are turned face down, it is impossible for anyone to successfully paper clip the centermost card!

Giant Balloon Reindeer

This is great for emphasizing team spirit and cooperation. Balloons are distributed throughout the audience. As the trainer moves through the room and picks up different balloons, he molds them together in a number of different animals until finally they are all assembled into a giant balloon reindeer!

6   *Tricks for Trainers*

The Dream Hat

"What is it?" is always the first question asked upon seeing this round piece of foam or felt. When creativity and problem solving are the emphasis, this prop demonstrates the subject very well by molding itself into twelve different hats!

Wanted

A column of want ads from the local newspaper is shown on both sides. The spectator can even examine it! A pair of scissors is used to cut the paper in two. It's really cut! A piece of paper flutters to the floor. Nevertheless, when the paper is opened, it's back in one piece again! This happens two other times until the trainer accidently cuts the paper at an angle. Now the ad column is restored at a right angle to itself!

Frustration

A pencil with a string attached is looped around the fingers of a spectator. The challenge is to remove the pencil without cutting the cord or breaking the pencil. It's fun to watch an entire group try to help! You'll probably need to show them how, as this classic puzzle is tough to figure out!

Multiplying Money

Seven coins are counted carefully by the volunteer and held securely in his hand. The trainer begins to find imaginary coins in the air throwing them into the closed hand of the volunteer. Upon counting his coins again, the spectator's coins have increased in number according to the number of coins tossed into his hand by the trainer!

Tricks for Trainers   7

This section contains magic that does not require special props. Many of the magic tricks in this section are actually performed with articles borrowed from the group.

Let's Fake a Deal!

In this game, the volunteer is given the choice of three envelopes in an attempt to win a prize. No matter which envelope is selected, she misses the best prizes and ends up with a consolation prize!

Prophesy In Review

The audience works with the trainer in a review of the subject. Eventually, nine squares on a flip chart are covered with index cards enumerating the main points.

The trainer mentions that she received a letter from a rather weird relative who believes that he is psychic. As one person from the audience reads the letter, another person follows the instructions stated in the letter with unbelievable results!

It is as though the author of the letter is in the seminar room....and all of the main emphases of the training are again reviewed during this unusual process!

Mindreading In Review

As the audience calls out summary points for the presentation, the trainer writes them on pieces of paper, folds the paper, and places them into a large manila envelope.

One person comes and selects one of the slips and secretly opens it so that only he sees the point written on the paper. Nevertheless, the trainer successfully tells the person holding the paper exactly which emphasis is on the paper!

 Tricks for Trainers 9

Dizzy Dollar

A dollar bill is shown clearly on both sides and then rolled into a funnel. A dime is dropped into the funnel. With no quick moves, the dollar is slowly unrolled and again shown on both sides. There is no trace of the dime!

Wallpaper Tear Repair

In the midst of the seminar, the trainer notices that a huge piece has been gouged out of the wallpaper in the room. The wallpaper has been actually peeled back from a spot and hangs loosely from the wall!

The trainer simply walks over to the spot and covers the gouge with her hand. Upon removing her hand, the wallpaper is as good as new!

A Generic Disappearance

Any item small enough to hold in your hand can be made to disappear!

The Pendulum

Each person in the seminar constructs a pendulum from a piece of string and a key. They hold the pendulums with the keys hanging loosely at the bottom. As the trainer makes suggestions, the pendulums are made to swing in a circle first, stop, and then swing in a straight line. Each person has no idea how the pendulum moves!

The suggestibility of the human mind is illustrated in a manner that won't soon be forgotten!

Fingertip Suggestibility

Each seminar member holds his fingertips apart. However, when the seminar leader begins suggesting that the fingertips are coming together, they do! All over the room!

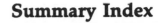
Wall Push

One of the smallest seminar members stands against a wall with arms outstretched — pushing against the wall. Other class members line up behind them — putting their hands on the shoulder of the person in front of them. Upon command, they push — attempting to push the front person into the wall. It can't be done!

Fingerlift

This demonstration illustrates the importance of attitude in success. As one member of the audience sits on a chair, four others stand around her. Using only two fingers each, these four people try and lift the person sitting on the chair with no success.

Now, the trainer begins to speak about the possibility of such an experiment. After the positive input from the trainer, the four lift the person in the chair effortlessly. The individual literally looks like she has indeed achieved weightlessness!

It's All In What You Know!

This dramatic demonstration has four men pitting their strength against one woman in an unbelievable demonstration of working smarter versus working harder!

Tricks for Trainers   11

This section has magic tricks designed to be first performed by the trainer and then taught to the members of the training class to help emphasize a point through hands-on involvement.

Paper Cuts

With a tongue in cheek lecture about the danger of paper cuts, the trainer sets up a demonstration.

A person holds a pencil between her hands while the trainer strikes it with the folded edge of a dollar bill.

Suddenly, the pencil breaks into two pieces upon being struck by the paper. It's sudden and dramatic! The explanation lends itself to helping an understanding of risk taking and the fears that keep us from achieving our potential.

The Trained Rubber Band

As the story is told, a trained rubber band performs tricks by jumping in a most unexpected manner!

Making George Smile

Everyone removes a dollar bill from their pocket. With only a little explanation from the trainer, each audience member suddenly looks at George Washington and sees him smiling broadly! By looking at the picture another way he suddenly looks angry! It's all a matter of perspective!

The Floating Hot Dog

The trainer helps each person make what appears to be a small hot dog float in the air right in front of their eyes!

The most unusual aspect of this demonstration is the fact that only the person floating the hot dog can see it!

It's a great demonstration for illustrating individual perspectives!

Personal Magnetism

Any straight object (pen, knife, ruler, etc.) can be made to float! Great for teaching how the details we don't see often cause us to be misled!

Future Forecast

The spectator has a completely free choice of three cards shown to her. In spite of this, the trainer has successfully predicted her choice beyond a shadow of a doubt!

Modern Art

What looks like simply a modern art design with no discernable purpose suddenly becomes an actual message when viewed from the proper perspective.

This comes complete with a guide for putting any message you want into the design to make your personalized message have impact with a handout that will be kept!

The Balancing

The trainer carefully (and with apparent skill) balances a cup on the EDGE of a plate! It totters at first and won't balance, but finally precariously stays on top of the plate's edge.

The explanation always brings laughs and helps the class understand how easily we can be fooled by situations we don't carefully examine.

The Mysterious Floating Silver Ball

The trainer stands with what appears to be a silver ball in his hand. The ball gently floats off the hand and rises up to meet the other waiting hand.

The audience is mesmerized by what they're seeing until they realize that the silver ball is the bowl of a soup ladle, the handle of which was stuck up the sleeve of the trainer!

Arm Alignment

The trainer complains about a pain in her shoulder. She wonders if maybe she didn't put it out of joint in her rather rigorous exercise program. She asks an audience member to gently push on the shoulder for her.

As someone does just that, there is suddenly a loud cracking sound that causes all in the room to jump!

When the trainer explains, she has a natural lead in to the subjects of perspective, cause and effect, assumptions or creative problem solving.

Tricks for Trainers   15

The Watch Drop

The trainer borrows a watch and ties it to a string —
hanging the string over a pencil. The trainer wants to
know how long the class believes it will take the watch
to drop and hit the floor. Unbelievable as it may seem,
the outcome of letting go of the string is completely unexpected — much to the relief of the person lending the
watch.

This is a great demonstration for illustrating the fear of
failure!

This section contains TEN audience-tested early bird exercises to use as people gather in the training room.

Each exercise has been designed to emphasize a different component necessary for maximizing creative thinking!

Exercise #1

The challenge is to drink out of a full can of pop without puncturing it, opening it, or destroying it in any way!

This is a great for discussing the importance of defining a problem before proceeding.

Exercise #2

Unscrambling the letters SECURA to form a common English word isn't as easy as it might first seem.

This is an excellent exercise for understanding how easily our minds can enter a rut and how difficult it can be to get out of those mental trenches.

Exercise #3

Finding the seven mistakes in this paragraph will take a very creative mind!

Exercise #4

Proving that a piece of wood is out of Noah's Ark will require careful attention to good communication skills.

Exercise #5

Unscrambling the letters PNLLEEEESSSSS will take the indispensable ingredient of persistence.

Exercise #6

Pushing a volunteer's head through a small bracelet will require attention to simplicity in order to achieve the solution.

Exercise #7

Finding the first letter in the word "_ E N Y" seems like it should be easy. However, once again our mind tends to become its own worst enemy.

Exercise #8

Only the person who doesn't limit himself with un-spoken rules will ever be able to prove the truth of a rather extraordinary paragraph.

Exercise #9

Finding more than one solution to this puzzle will encourage group members to not always look for just "the right answer."

Exercise #10

Duplicating the unbelievable sculpture in this exercise will challenge each person in the group to work beyond the first few failed attempts.

This section contains ELEVEN of the greatest braintwisters of all time!

They are great for putting a mental break in a seminar and for illustrating many different emphases about how our thought processes work.

They really help to maintain a creative and interactive environment!

Braintwister #1

As a volunteer stands on a chair, the trainer claims to be able to get her off the chair before the trainer counts to three. No physical force is involved in this challenge. How will she do it?

Braintwister #2

Holding two American coins in his closed hand, the trainer claims that the value of the coins totals six cents. How can it be since he also states that one of the coins is NOT a nickel?

Braintwister #3

The trainer claims to be able to toss a paper match high in the air and have it come down and land on its edge!

Braintwister #4

Showing the group a column of numbers, the class is challenged to add the numbers in their heads. The end result is always way off even though the addition is not difficult at all!

　　Tricks for Trainers　19

Braintwister #5

A transparency with a cute picture of a rabbit and top hat is shown to the group. The simple message on the hat is read by the group. Nevertheless, few members read it correctly!

Braintwister #6

The seminar leader shows, through the use of a transparency, how by simply depositing and withdrawing money in a bank account, money can be made! Can figures lie?

Braintwister #7

In order to slip a book of matches under a full can of pop without touching the can, each person will need to think with maximum creativity!

Braintwister #8

How would you drop a light bulb on a cement floor without breaking the bulb? You can't wrap the bulb in anything or put anything on the floor to cushion the drop. The bulb must be dropped from a height of at least five feet!

Braintwister #9

With a rope held by two people and stretched across the front of the training room, a solid bracelet is threaded onto the rope. The trainer challenges the group to come up with at least two ways to pull the bracelet right off the rope without either person letting go of her end of the rope.

Braintwister #10

Grabbing both of the strings hanging from the ceiling will require real ingenuity. The strings are too far apart to reach the ends at the same time!

Braintwister #11

This tabloid story can't possibly be true! Can you figure out why?

 Tricks for Trainers 21

Section One

This first section contains magic that requires special props. Most of them can be made from materials readily available or you can call Resources for Organizations, Inc. for availability.

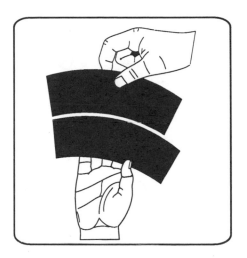

This routine utilizes two boomerangs produced with a reusable writing surface. It is particularly effective when used in comparing two components, since either boomerang can be shown longer or shorter than the other one . . . or both can be shown as being the same size.

Use the enclosed templates to make the boomerangs out of heavy cardboard or thin plywood. By covering the surface of these boomerangs with white contact paper, you can make the surface re-usable using dry erase markers.

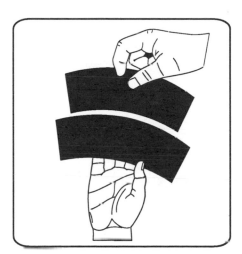

In showing the boomerangs different sizes, hold them up with one resting on top and above the other. For maximum impact, line up either the right or left edges of the boomerangs. This makes the size difference more dramatic.

Now lower the one on top so that it is now the one on the bottom, and it will become the longer one of the pair.

Whichever one you put on the bottom will always appear longer than the other one.

In order to show them the same size, place the boomerang that is actually shorter on top of the other one and fan them slightly so that the smaller boomerang is on the inside of the fan.

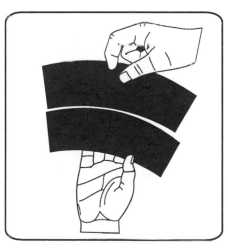

Tricks for Trainers   25

Boomerang Template

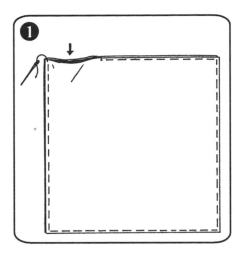

Anything wrapped up in the handkerchief disappears!

In preparation, you will need to take two matching bandanna style handkerchiefs and sew the edges together with the exception of about 1/3 of the top left corner. This allows you to be able to reach in between the two handkerchiefs.

Many bandannas have manufacturer's printing on one side. Position that printing so that it can help you locate the opening.

In order to use the handkerchief to make an item disappear, bring the four corners of the handkerchief up into your right or left hand so that the handkerchief forms a bag.

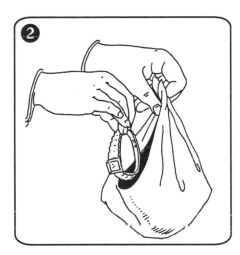

Take the item you wish to vanish and place it into the handkerchief actually placing it into the opening between the two handkerchiefs.

Someone can actually now feel the item in the handkerchief right up until the disappearance.

Shake the handkerchief out and show the handkerchief on both sides. The item appears to have disappeared!

Be sure to keep track of the opening from the beginning of the routine so that when you open the handkerchief the opening remains at the top and the item can't fall out!

After the article has vanished, casually put the handkerchief away.

You can also have a duplicate article hidden somewhere in the room so that after the disappearance it can "reappear" elsewhere in the room.

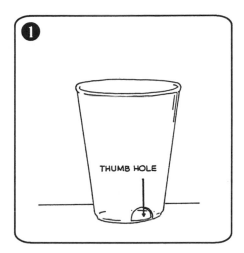

A clear plastic glass is placed on a book and covered with a handkerchief. The littlest child in the audience is able to lift it from the book, but you can make it so that the strongest adult will not be able to!

You will need a plastic glass that is fluted enough to cause it to be almost opaque.

You need to make a hole with a hot needle at the bottom of one side of the glass. This hole needs to be large enough so that your thumb can be comfortably inserted and withdrawn from the hole.

Your audience must never be aware of this hole!

It won't be hard to keep the hole hidden due to the design of the glass. Just keep the hole to the backside away from the audience and you can even wrap your fingers around the bottom of the glass while holding it.

Begin by showing the glass, keeping it in motion so that no one has a chance to study it.

Now you can fill the cup with tissues. This will also help hide the hole from the audience.

Place the glass on a book with the secret hole again away from the audience. Cover the glass with a handkerchief and use the book as a tray to lift the glass away from the table.

Have anyone try to lift the glass away from the book, gripping it at the top through the cloth of the handkerchief. It's easy.

While you hold the book from the back edge with your thumb on top and fingers underneath the book, use your other hand to slide the glass back so that your right hand thumb can enter the hole in the back of the glass and press the glass down on the book.

Now have them try and lift the glass again. With your thumb in the hole, they will not succeed!

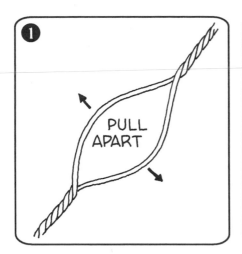

1 PULL APART

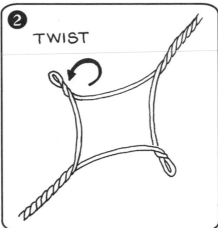

2 TWIST

3 TWIST TO FORM TIGHT FAKE ENDS

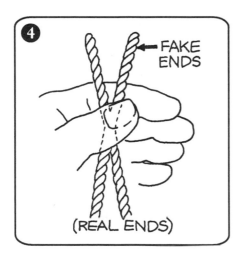

4 FAKE ENDS

(REAL ENDS)

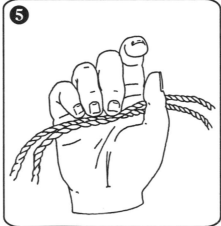

5

Two pieces of string are shown and placed in a spectator's hand. As you pull on the ends of the string, the spectator will feel the string actually join together in his hand!

Although this does work with string, for better visibility you might choose a piece of yarn approximately three feet long. You will notice that a piece of yarn is actually many little yarn threads wrapped around each other.

Before you perform this great trick find the middle of your piece of yarn and use your hands to loosen the fibers by twisting your fingers in opposite directions so that the fibers loosen.

Take half of the yarn fibers in each hand and gently pull them apart. When you let the fibers go, you will find them springing back and making what looks like two ends in the middle of the long piece of yarn. Twist the two fake ends you've just made so that they are each tighter looking.

Hold the yarn between your thumb and index finger so that your fingers hide the secret joint you've just created. It should now look like you're holding two pieces of yarn.

Lay the fake ends in the hand of a volunteer and close his hand around the ends so that he doesn't see the joint. The other ends of the yarn should hang out either side of his hand.

Pull on the ends of the string hanging out of his hand and he will feel the other ends come together in his hand!

An additional idea concerns preparing the yarn ahead of time and having it on your training table. Prepare as above and then tie the two halves of the yarn together in an overhand knot so that the knot forms at the secret joint. Then you pick up the yarn and untie it whenever you're ready to illustrate your point.

String Sensation -An Alternate Presentation

This presentation is perfect for illustrating how we need to "pull together" in order to accomplish a project.

The string for this particular presentation needs to be about 30 inches long. Prepare it just like in the first version so that the two "fake ends" show above your hand.

Proceed as in the first version to show the audience that you have two pieces of string in your hand.

Invite two volunteers to join you up front and have them stand one on either side of you. Indicate that you will attempt to hold one end of each string in your hand while each of the volunteers pull on the other ends.

With one hand alone, you will resist the strength of two people! Really build this up!

Give one of the real ends to each volunteer and have them pull while you hold the other two "ends" in your hand. Encourage them to wrap the string around their hand at least once to make sure they keep a good grip on the string!

Make a show of moistening your fingertips, etc. as you prepare for this feat of strength.

As they pull on their ends, grimace as you appear to be struggling. Finally relax and turn to your audience to ask if they would like to know how you do this trick. Of course, they would.

Open your hand to show the one piece of string and the two people pulling against each other!

In many organizations, that is the picture. People aren't pulling together...but pulling against each other!

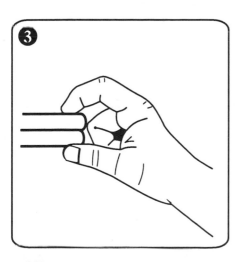

Two slates are shown blank on both sides. They are placed face to face with a piece of chalk placed between them. When the slates are held up to the ear of a spectator, they can actually hear the chalk writing! When the slates are separated, a message of your choice appears on the slates!

Two unprepared school slates and a piece of chalk are needed to perform this excellent routine.

The secret is to learn how to apparently show both sides of the slates clean while hiding the message on one side of a slate.

Write a message on one side of a slate and place that slate down on the table with the writing face up. Place the other slate on top of the first slate so that the message is hidden between the two slates Pick up the slates together in one hand with the secret writing on the bottom slate hidden between the two slates. You should hold the slates with your thumb on top and other fingers underneath. You should grip the slates on one of its longer edges. The long edge you grip should be the closest edge to your body. In your other hand, you have the eraser.

Wipe the top slate in your hand and then turn your wrist and wipe the one side of the lower slate. Then turn your wrist back to its original position with the thumb on top.

Reach over the top of the slates around to the front with your free hand and grip the front edge of the lower slate, pulling it forward and away from the upper slate. At the same time that you're pulling the slate out, you let the long edge of that slate closest to you fall down towards the table. You flip this lower slate writing side down onto the table.

Finish up by using your eraser to wipe both sides of the slate remaining in your hand — letting it flip down onto the slate that's already on the table.

Take a piece of chalk and place it on the upper slate lifting the upper slate off the table. Take the other slate and lift it off the table (keeping the writing face down) and place it on top of the chalk so that the chalk is now between the two slates.

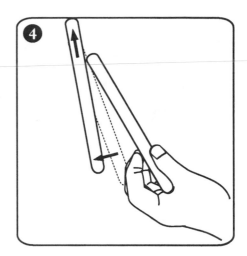

Wait a while and then lift off the top slate (remember that the writing is on this slate so keep the writing face down) and check to see if the chalk has done any writing yet.

Of course, you won't see any writing on the lower slate. Replace the top slate back over the chalk and hold the slates up to someone's ear. Ask if they hear anything.

As you raise the slates up to their ear turn both slates over in your hand so that the lower slate is now on top.

Hold it by their ear for a little while and then use your fingernail to gently scratch on one of the slates. It will sound just like the chalk is beginning to write!

Act excited and look again. Because you turned the slates over, the writing will now be face up on the slate!

The secret to these moves is acting like nothing is happening while you are cleaning the slates. Don't act suspicious or stiff. You are just cleaning some slates. In the mind of the audience, the magic doesn't really begin until the slates are put together with the chalk between. Only you know that at that point the work is over.

An additional idea might be to actually have some words on one or more of the slates at the beginning so that you can allude to the word as you erase it — setting up for the appearance of the final message! These words can easily be part of your presentation.

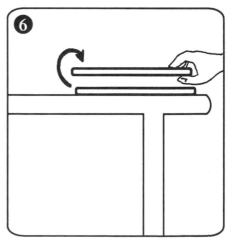

Practice until you don't need to think about what you are doing, and then you'll be able to do it casually and no one in your audience will become suspicious. Remember that they don't know what's going to happen until you've put the chalk between the slates and the dirty work is over.

After showing the slates blank per the instructions, pick up the slate that really is blank on both sides and begin to tell your story:

Once there were two electronic stores located right across the street from each other. Needless to say, they were locked in fierce competition trying to outdo the other one.

One day one of the owners got the idea to run what he thought to be a great promotion. He simply put a large sign in the window that read:

$25
TV's

(As you say these last words, print the words on the slate you're holding. Now pick up the other slate from the table being careful to keep the side with the secret message away from the audience. Place the slates together with the messages face-to-face as you continue with your story.)

Not to be outdone the other very creative owner made a sign of his own. He simply put a sign in his window which said:

$25
TV's
FIXED
HERE!

(As you say these last lines turn the slate so that this message now shows. You had secretly put this message on one side of the slate before the presentation began.)

Sawing A Person In Half *(diagram)*

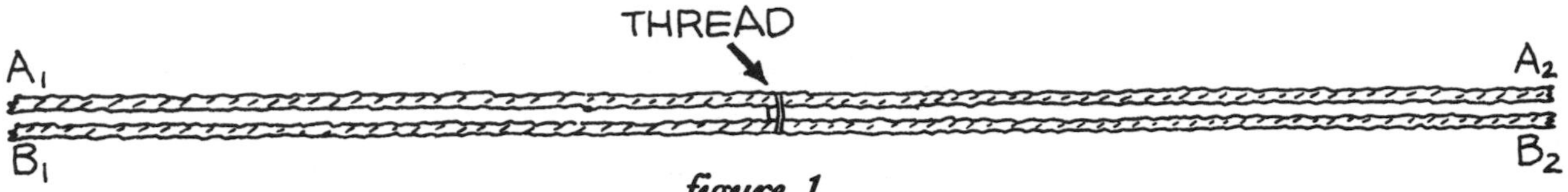
THREAD
A1
A2
B1
B2

figure 1.

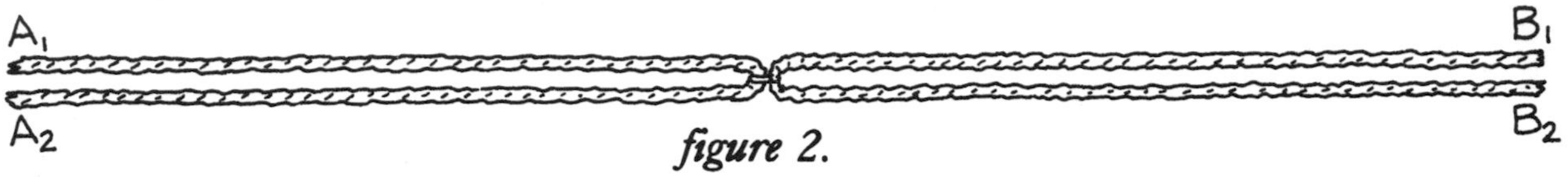
A1
B1
A2
B2

figure 2.

Two spectators help to tie ropes around the waist of a third audience member. As the ropes are pulled, the spectator can feel them tighten around her waist! Yet when the ropes are pulled quickly, they visibly melt right through the waist of the volunteer!

You will need two pieces of rope each at least eight feet long. You will also need a piece of thin white thread.

Before presenting this routine take a piece of thread and tie it around the center of both ropes as in figure 1.

Now fold the ropes so that both ends of the same rope are together as in figure 2. The ropes are held together by the thread. Place this rope on your table.

When you're ready to perform, get three people up to help you. Pick up the rope from your table so that the thread holding the ropes together is concealed by your hand. The ropes are still in the condition pictured in figure 2 above.

Stand behind the person you're going to saw in half and have a volunteer stand on each side of her. The thread as seen in figure 2 is now hidden by the volunteer's body. Hand one end of rope B to the volunteer on that side and one end of rope A to the other volunteer and ask them to tie a simple overhand knot around the waist of the person you're going to saw in half. This tying of the knot will unknowingly cause them to exchange their ends with each other.

After they have tied the simple knot give each of them another end of the rope you're still holding. The other A end goes to the person you gave the A end to before and the B end goes to the person you gave the B end to before.

Have them pull on their ends and the thread will break and the ropes will appear to pass right through your volunteer.

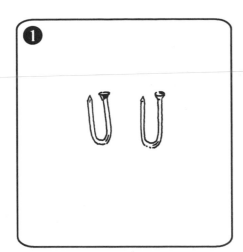

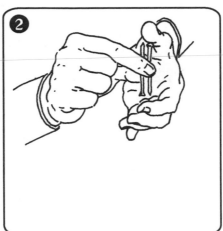

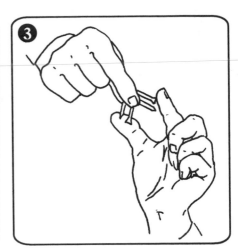

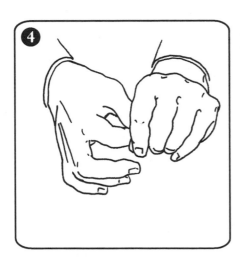

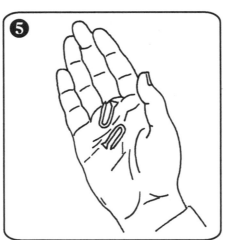

This trick was contributed by Tom Ogden, Hollywood, CA. Used with permission.

Picking up two nails, you bend them in your bare hand!

In preparation, you will need to take two nails and bend them completely in half. The nails must be bent so that the two halves of the nail are parallel to each other.

You will need to learn how to hold these nails between your two fingers as in the drawing. Line them up so that they look like two straight nails. Your thumb and index finger hide the joint where the two nails meet at their centers.

To get in this position obtain a box such as the type used for carrying a bar of soap during travel.

Into this box place about a dozen ordinary nails as well as your two prepared nails.

Begin by opening the box and handing out a few nails to members of the group as you talk about your upcoming demonstration. While they are examining their nails, reach into the box and with one hand get your two prepared nails into position.

Once in position, close the box and put it aside. Use your other hand to put your index and thumb on the top and bottom of the nails and begin to act as though you're bending them.

After bending them just a little, put them both into one hand and continue to squeeze them. Finally, drop them onto the table in their totally bent condition! Pick up one of the nails and put it back into your pocket, but let them try and bend the other one. You don't want them to have both nails in their hands to experiment with how to hold them.

This is also very effective when the spectator "bends" the nails in their own hand. The trainer simply takes the nails from his own hand "bending" them in the process and places them in the hand of the volunteer closing their fingers around the nails so they can's see that they are already bent.

We are all stronger than we think!

 Tricks for Trainers 41

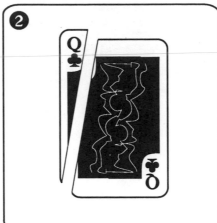

TAPE HERE

Three large cards are shown with the odd card in the middle of the spread. The cards are turned slowly over and when the center card is removed, the card contains a special message for introducing the topic of the training!

Take two similar cards (same color) and one of contrasting color (and a picture card if possible). Regular size cards can be used although jumbo cards provide much greater visibility.

Place the three cards in a face-up fan so that the indexes show on each.

Make sure that the top left hand corner of the center card does not extend above the top of the bottom card. Take a pencil and lightly trace the left edge of the middle card so that you know where it belongs when placed on top of the bottom card in the fan.

You are now going to cut away all of the middle card that the audience doesn't see when the cards are fanned.

In other words, all of the middle card that is underneath the uppermost card must be marked and then cut away.

Once you have cut away the card, you place what's left of the middle card back onto the bottom card in the fan, using your previous pencil lines to guide you. Then use a piece of transparent tape UNDERNEATH this card piece to hinge it along its left edge.

You now will need a fourth card with a back that matches the other three in your fan. Cut a piece of index card so that it covers the face of the playing card and glue it in place. On this card, you will print your message.

Insert the message card, angling it underneath the flap piece of card lining up the top edges of the cards. Place the only remaining card on top of the fan and display it to your audience.

It should look just like it did when you first fanned the three cards in preparing for this routine.

Turn the fan face down and remove what appears to be the middle card (it is really the message card).

If you want to be fancy, you can close the other two cards into a tighter fan hiding the flap piece. You could then show the faces of these two cards since the flap piece would be hidden. Place these two cards aside and dramatically reveal the message on the card in your hand!

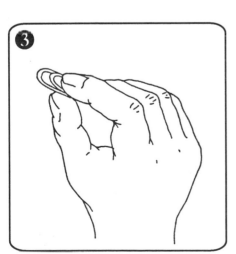

Five playing cards are glued together in an overlapping row to prove that no manipulation of the cards is possible. Nevertheless, when the cards are turned face down, it is impossible for anyone to successfully paper clip the centermost card!

Take four playing cards of one color and one of the contrasting color and place them in an overlapping row so that the index of each card is visible and so that the contrasting card is the middle card in the spread.

After arranging the cards as stated above, glue them together so that they become a permanent set of overlapping cards.

Now turn the cards face down and take a paper clip, challenging anyone to paper clip the center card (the odd card).

It looks so easy. But it's not!

It's all a matter of perspective!

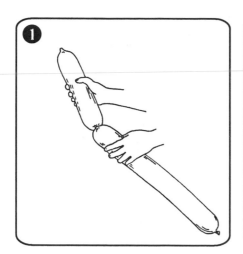
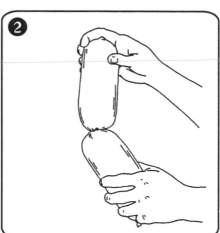
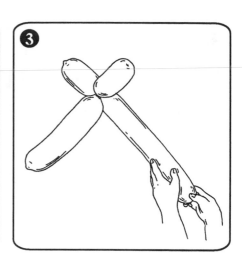

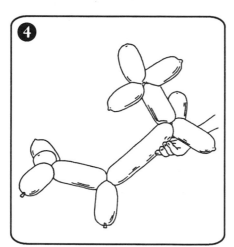
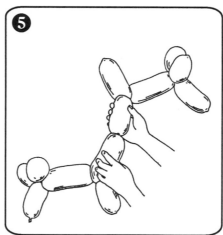
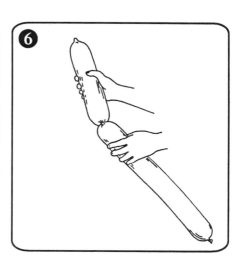

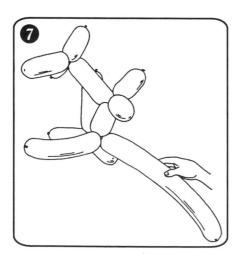
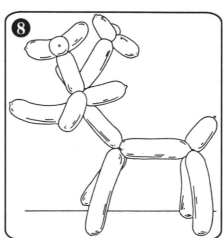

This is great for emphasizing team spirit and cooperation. Balloons are distributed throughout the audience. As the trainer moves through the room and picks up different balloons, he molds them together into a number of different animals until finally they are all assembled into a giant balloon reindeer!

The giant reindeer is built from eight balloons called "airship balloons." Four of the balloons are known as 340's and four of the balloons are known as 312's. The first digit in those numbers tells you the diameter of the balloon when inflated (3") while the last two numbers tell you its length (either 12" or 40").

You can find these balloons by calling a party supply store in your town or calling Resources for Organizations, Inc. for availability.

Inflate all eight balloons. **BE CAREFUL TO NOT OVERINFLATE!**

Leave from an inch to two inches uninflated on the shorter balloons and from two to three inches uninflated on the longer balloons.

Take one of the long balloons, which will eventually be the main part of the reindeer's antlers, and at about 12" from one end twist one section to the right and the other section to the left. Put the twisted section under your arm to keep it from untwisting (figure 1).

Now take one of the small balloons and twist it in the same manner to make two bubbles in the balloon of equal size (figure 2).

Bend and twist the groove in the short balloon around the groove in the long balloon until it looks like figure 3.

In the same manner, add a small balloon 12" from the other end of the long balloon. Then add one more small balloon only six inches from one end of your original long balloon.

Now you should have what looks like either a dachshund or a giraffe depending upon how you hold it!

Tricks for Trainers   47

Add one more small balloon six inches from the other end of the long balloon (the end that doesn't already have two small balloons), and the result should look like figure 4 — a two-headed dog!

Take the long balloon and place a twist in it approximately 10" from the UNKNOTTED end of the balloon. This should now look like figure 6.

Place the twisted antler section into the twist you just made and twist these balloons together (figure 7).

Finally, take the remaining two long balloons and prepare to twist them in place to make the legs of the reindeer.

Approximately 8" back from the antlers on the long balloon (the body) make a twist. Now take another long balloon and make a twist in it right in the middle of its length. Twist this long balloon into the twist you first made in the main body of the reindeer.

Then 10" or so back from this first set of legs add the last long balloon in the same manner. You should leave a small tail on the reindeer.

Bend and shape the balloons until the reindeer looks like figure 8!

"What is it?" Is always the first question asked upon seeing this round piece of material. When creativity and problem solving are the emphases, this prop demonstrates the subject very well by molding itself into twelve different hats!

The prop itself can be cut either out of 1/2" foam or two pieces of heavy felt can be sewn together. The darker colors of black or gray work best for displaying the hat.

The hat ring has an outside diameter of 16" with an inside hole measuring 5 1/2".

In the directions which follow, you will find many hats that can be made by twisting this ring of material. However, as you become more familiar with the material, both you and your trainees will have great fun creating new designs!

The Cowboy

This is the simplest type of figure. With no folding at all, the ring is placed on the head, the brim being turned up at the front. The hat is placed far enough back on the head so that the supposed crown of the hat is hidden from the audience.

The Choir Boy

Pull your head through the ring of material so that it rests on your shoulders. You will find that you now look like you're wearing the top of a choir robe.

The Revolutionary Soldier

This hat forms the foundation for several to follow. To make this hat, refer to the illustrations.

Have the hat in the hand, as in 1. Reach down through the hole and grasp the front edge at X, and then pull X up through the hole as indicated by the arrows in 2.

Place the hat on the head as in the final illustration.

Tricks for Trainers   51

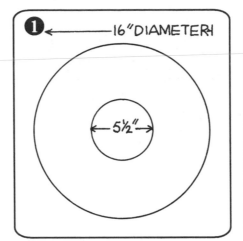

❶ ←— 16"DIAMETER→

5½"

❷ THE COWBOY

❸ THE CHOIR BOY

❹ BASEBALL HAT

❺ THE SHIP'S CAPTAIN

❻ NAPOLEAN'S HAT

The Ladies Bonnet

Take The Revolutionary Soldier Hat, placing it on the head from the back as illustrated. The neck hides the rolled part of the hat and only the "bonnet" part shows.

The Nun

Taking the Revolutionary Soldier Hat, place it like the Ladies Bonnet, only insert your face from the back of the unit. The bonnet will now be around your face with the rolled part forming part of the nun's habit below your neck.

The Silly Hat

For those days you feel particularly silly, this one is great.

Take the Revolutionary Soldier Hat, placing it on the head as illustrated.

By folding back the material on the side of the face, a Pied Piper's Hat results.

The Baseball Hat

Again taking the Revolutionary Soldier Hat, place it on the head with the rolled part of the hat to the front. The material at the sides of the hat should be sticking up into the air rather than down over your ears. Flatten the rolled part out by loosening the roll. This front part then becomes the bill of the hat.

By folding down the material on the sides of the hat, you have a baseball hat with "wings!"

The Ship's Captain

This hat now forms the basis of others to follow. Take the ring of material and fold both sides up in the inner circle. Set the hat on your head as in the illustration.

 Tricks for Trainers 53

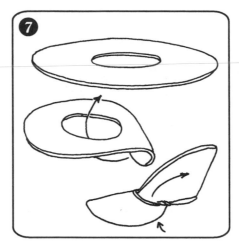

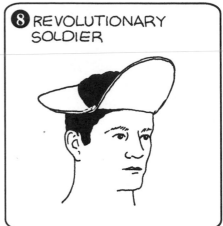

8 REVOLUTIONARY SOLDIER

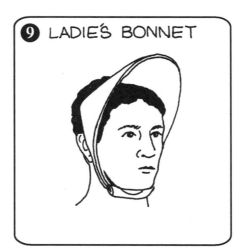

9 LADIE'S BONNET

10 THE NUN

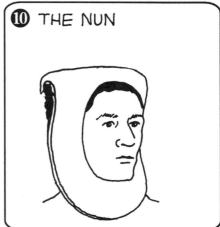

11 GRADUATION CAP

12 SILLY HAT

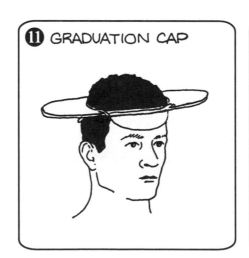

Napoleon's Hat

Take the Ship's Captain hat and turn it on your head so that it appears as in the illustration. A simple placing of one hand into the front of your shirt gives you the "Napoleon look."

College Graduation Hat

By turning the Ship's Captain hat upside down on your head and flattening out the top of the hat, a mortarboard appearance can be achieved. Work with it in front of a mirror until you can see it.

The Pirate's Hat

This last one is the most difficult one to describe. Push some of the material through the hole in the hat. This material will eventually be the pirate's patch.

Put the hat on your head with this pulled through piece of material covering one of your eyes. Look in a mirror with the other one and shape the remainder of the material on your head until a Pirates's Hat comes into view. The bulk of the material will simply rise up behind your head.

Other Ideas

Other hats are waiting to be found. Can you find a Rembrandt's Artist hat? Mickey Mouse ears? A Court Jester's hat? Others? There are many more waiting to be found in this simple ring of material — The Hat Of The Imagination.

Tricks for Trainers   55

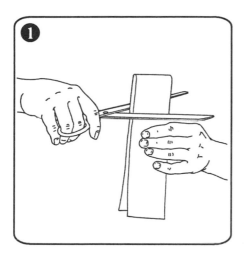

A column of want ads from the local newspaper is shown on both sides. The spectator can even examine it! A pair of scissors is used to cut the paper in two. It's really cut! A piece of the paper flutters to the floor. Nevertheless, when the paper is opened, it's back in one piece again! This happens two other times until the trainer accidently cuts the paper at an angle. Now the ad is restored at a right angle to itself!

Cut some want ad column-wide strips about eight inches long. Coat both sides with a coating of rubber cement. After the rubber cement dries, dust both sides with talcum powder.

Take one of the strips and experiment. Fold the strip in half. Then take a pair of scissors and cut the folded end off as in figure 1. The folded end will flutter to the floor. Don't put your scissor blades between the folded halves but rather simply cut the folded end off by having one of the blades going behind the papers and the other in front of them.

Let go of one of the ends you're holding in your other hand and allow the strip to unfold. Your audience will see that it has already restored itself!

You can now fold it and do it again — cutting off more from the bottom of the paper.

If you separate the two halves, simply align them again and clip another piece off. They will be joined again.

If you cut the paper at an angle, the paper will restore itself at an angle. Then simply clip the angle straight and the paper will again be straightly restored.

Of course you have already realized that you can't PULL on the two ends after a cut has been made. The paper would then pull apart at the cut. But if you let one end drop after each cut and then fold it back up, you won't need to worry about the halves coming apart.

Raise the paper higher so the reader can see it - it should be cut across.

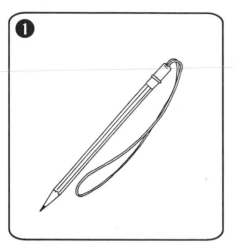

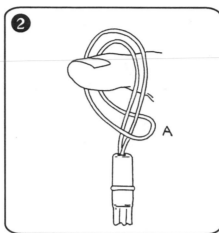

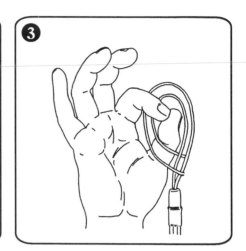

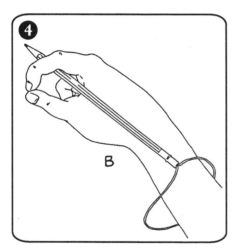

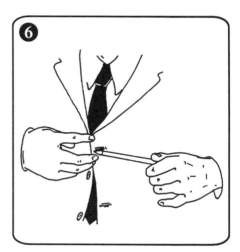

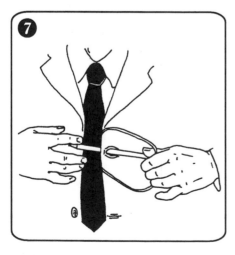

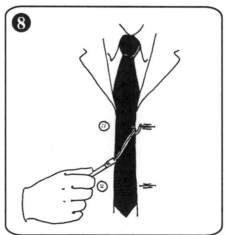

A pencil with a string attached is looped around the fingers of a spectator. The challenge is to remove the pencil without cutting the cord or breaking the pencil. It's fun to watch an entire group try to help! You'll probably need to show them how as this classic puzzle is tough to figure out!

You will need to take a pencil and drill a small hole in the eraser end of the pencil. Take a string and thread it through the hole, tying it into a loop.

It is important that the loop is just barely too short to slip around the opposite end of the pencil!

In order to put this puzzle onto a person's fingers, follow the diagrams. First, make a loop with the string over the pencil as in figure A and put the spectator's thumb and forefinger through this loop. Have her touch the tip of her thumb to the tip of her index finger so as to form a circle. The challenge now is to remove the pencil from the hand without separating the thumb and finger, breaking the pencil or cutting the string!

Try it yourself before reading further.

To get the pencil free, take the string at point "A" in figure 1 and pull the loop up over the hand and up the wrist far enough so you can pull the pencil out through the circle formed by your thumb and finger. Then pull the pencil and string down over your hand and off as in figure B.

AN ADDITIONAL IDEA might include threading the pencil through a button hole as shown below. This also makes a challenging problem!

     Tricks for Trainers   59

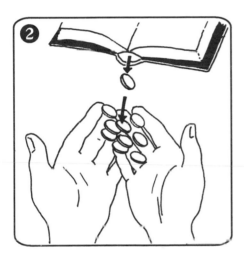

Seven coins are counted carefully by the volunteer and held securely in his hand. The trainer begins to find imaginary coins in the air, throwing them into the closed hand of the volunteer. Upon counting his coins again, the spectator's coins have increased in number of coins tossed into his hand by the trainer!

Although this routine is not difficult to do, it is the longest routine in this book. In spite of the fact that you can shorten and simplify it to fit your situation, the routine will be presented in its entirety. It has proven itself in hundreds of seminars for over ten years.

A Multiplying Coin Tray helps to make this trick possible, but if you don't have one the routine can also be done with a small hard covered book. The book must have a spine that opens up into a tube when the book is opened.

Begin by placing seven quarters in your right pocket, another quarter in your left pocket, and two additional quarters in the spine of the book or the secret compartment of the tray.

The tray looks like it might be an ashtray or a coaster for a drink. By all means try and use it for something on your training supply table rather than just having it sitting there looking like a magic tray.

If you don't have the tray, you will open your book and use it as a tray in all of the descriptions that follow.

Select a volunteer from the audience and indicate that you want to play "THE YES GAME!" All the volunteer needs to do is to answer "yes" to every question you are about to ask. He is to never answer "no" although you will try and trick him into saying "no." The other audience members will be the judges.

Ask him if he understands. He should say "yes." Compliment him on how quick he is.

Show him the seven quarters from your pocket and place them onto the tray (or the open book).

  Tricks for Trainers 61

Ask him if he believes there are seven quarters on the tray. He should answer "yes," but have him count them anyway. Pour them into his cupped hands so that the secret opening of the tray does not dump the extra quarters yet. If you are using the book, simply pick the quarters up off the book and have him count them back onto the book or tray one at a time.

Ask him if he's going to forget how to play this game. He should answer "yes." This will bring a good response from the rest of the group.

Have him hold his hands out and pour all of the quarters including the secret quarters into his hands. Have him close his hands tightly together.

Suddenly act as though you see something in the air. Reach up and grab it.

Ask him if he sees the quarter. He should say "yes."

Suddenly notice another quarter behind the volunteer's ear. Bring it out, show it to him, and make it a boomerang coin. Sail the coin around the room, following it with your eyes and have it land back in his hand.

Ask him if he felt that one land. Again, he should say "yes."

Finally, explain to him that the last quarter is the most difficult. Reach into the pocket that has the real quarter and hide it in your hand. However, withdraw your hand as though you are holding an imaginary quarter between your thumb and index finger. Your other fingers hide the real quarter.

Tell him that you are going to throw this last quarter at his foot. He will feel it go in his foot, up his leg, down his arm and into his hand.

Throw it at his foot and wait.

Ask him if he felt it go in his foot. He should say "yes." Ask him if he felt it go up his leg. He should say "yes." Ask him if he felt it go down his arm. He should say "yes."

Reflect out loud for a moment about how many coins that means he should have in his hands. Think hard and then after mental calculation say "ten!"

"Let's count them," you say.

Grab your tray (or book) and have him count them onto the tray. He will only have nine (remember you still have one hidden in your hand).

Ask him if he has another one. He should say "yes."

Suddenly, you notice something. Have him stand still and touch his nose with the hand that has the hidden quarter.

Hold your tray under that hand and let the quarter fall onto the tray from your hand. It should look like you shook his nose and the quarter fell out!

Thank your volunteer for his kind help!

Tricks for Trainers   63

TRICKS FOR TRAINERS

Section Two

This section contains magic that does not require special props. Many of the magic tricks in this section are actually performed with articles borrowed from the group.

In this game, the volunteer is given the choice of three envelopes in an attempt to win a prize. No matter which envelope is selected, they miss the best prizes and end up with a consolation prize!

In preparing for this excellent routine, take three number ten OPAQUE envelopes and number them each with large numerals — either 1, 2 or 3.

Take three 8 1/2 x 11 sheets of paper and describe on each one a different truly great prize that anyone would enjoy winning (i.e. an all-expense paid trip, a car, a video entertainment center, etc.). Fold these into thirds and place one into each of the envelopes. After placing the paper in the envelope tuck in the envelope's flap as though you were getting ready to mail the envelope.

Now take three more 8 1/2 x 11 sheets of paper and describe on each one the same prize (one that you're willing to give away). This prize can be anything from a keychain, to a potato, to a round of applause from the other trainers.

Fold these into thirds and insert them into the envelopes but on the outside of the flaps (not underneath the flaps).

You are now ready to begin!

Invite one of the trainers to play a game for a great prize! Show her the envelopes and invite her to choose either envelope number 1, 2 or 3.

Hand her the envelope and indicate that she should withdraw her prize description. She will of course withdraw the paper she first sees in the envelope (the one on the outside of the flap). Take the envelope back from her so she can't look further.

Before having her open her paper, suggest that you look to see what she didn't win.

Take the other two envelopes and one at a time open the flap and withdraw the innermost paper reading the prize she lost.

Tricks for Trainers   67

Finally, have her read the prize she did win.

Congratulate her as you send her back to her seat with her cherished prize!

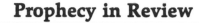
The audience will work with the trainer in a review of the subject. Eventually, nine squares on a flip chart are covered with index cards enumerating the main points.

The trainer mentions that she received a letter from a rather weird relative who believes that he is psychic. As one person from the audience reads the letter, another person follows the instructions stated in the letter with unbelievable results! It is as though the author of the letter is in the seminar room and all of the main emphases are reviewed again during this unusual process!

To prepare for this routine take nine index cards and number them 1-9 in their upper left hand corner. On the back of card #6, you will need to print a message that reads "I knew that you'd finish on this card!"

Print each one of the summary points on the numbered side of separate cards.

IMPORTANT: Those summary points with an even number of letters must be printed on the odd numbered cards. Those cards with an odd number of letters must be printed on the even numbered cards.

Now stick the cards on a flip chart in the following order:

1	2	3
4	5	6
7	8	9

After using the cards for reviewing your summary emphases, mention a letter you received from a rather odd friend of yours. The friend believes he's psychic. You now give the following letter to a person in the audience to read as another person goes to the flipchart and follows the letter's directions.

NOTE: You can rewrite this letter in longhand if you want to achieve the maximum dramatic impact!

Dear (Your Name),

I know you doubt my psychic abilities. But I tell you it's true! It's a gift I have. I'm full of it. Allow me to demonstrate!

I am concentrating on one of the cards you have before you! Follow my instructions carefully, and I will lead you to discover the card that's in my mind.

Place your finger on any of the cards you choose. You can change your mind if you want but finally settle on one card only. Please stand to the side so others can see.

All you need to understand is that when you are told to move, you can move your finger from one card to any of its immediate neighbors, so long as you jump in an orderly fashion, either horizontally or vertically. Diagonal jumps and other odd moves are not permitted. However, you can change your direction as you jump as often as you please which gives you freedom to roam over the cards pretty much as you like.

Do you understand? All right let's begin!

First, move your finger once for each letter in the word on the card on which your finger now rests. In other words, if the word on your selected card has four letters, you will move your finger from one card to another four times.

Please remove card #2. That is not the card I'm thinking about.

Did I tell you that I would also know how you are moving your finger? Well now you know. Card #2 is no longer part of the board. As soon as a card is removed, you must go around the empty space left by its removal. You are not permitted to go through an empty space.

Seven is a near perfect number. So please move your finger seven times. . . and then remove card #7. It is no longer needed.

 　　　Tricks for Trainers　　71

Now move your finger six times. Remember no diagonal moves and no moves through areas that no longer have a card.

You can remove card #9 and proceed to move yet another six times.

Now remove card #3. We are done with that card. It is not the card on which my mind is focused.

One more time. . . move your finger six times and remove the card #1. It is gone!

Now take your finger and carefully move five times. Remember, you can change directions while you move. Remove card #4. It is not the card of my choice.

Now move four times. We're going to speed things up just a little. Remove card #8.

Only two possibilities remain. Either card #5 or card #6 is my predicted card. To find out which one, move your finger three times. You are left with the card of my choice. Go ahead and remove card #5. You'll find that I knew you'd stop on card #6. You doubt that I knew? Go ahead and turn card #6 over.

Thank you for moving your finger just as I predicted. You helped me prove my rather unusual power!

Your friend,

Dr. Albert Shyster

As the audience calls out summary points for the presentation, the trainer writes them on pieces of paper, folds the paper, and places them into a large manila envelope.

One person comes and selects one of the slips and secretly opens it so that only he sees the point written on the paper. Nevertheless, the trainer successfully tells the person holding the paper exactly which emphasis is on the paper!

The secret is so simple that people will skip over it as a possibility as they try and reconstruct the routine!

After you genuinely write the first person's contribution on a piece of paper and place it in the envelope, you do the same with the second person's contribution.

However, after the second contribution, you only write the second person's contribution on all the remaining slips even though you act as though you are writing the contribution just being made!

Naturally at the end of the routine, the person will most likely pick a paper with the second person's contribution written on it. . . however, even if he picks the contribution of the first person, you will appear even more amazing by missing just a little and then correcting yourself!

Tricks for Trainers   73

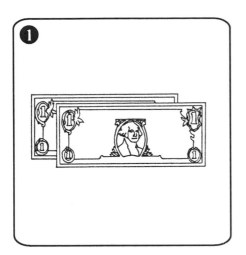

POCKET OPENING

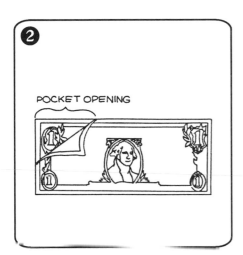

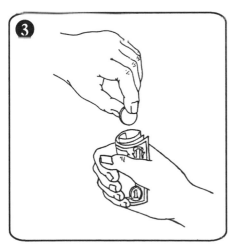

A dollar is shown clearly on both sides and then rolled into a funnel. A dime is dropped into the funnel. With no quick moves, the dollar is slowly unrolled and again is shown on both sides. There is no trace of the dime.

You will need to make a special dollar by using two dollar bills and some rubber cement. Take the two dollar bills and place them on top of each other with both having the green side down and both being rightside up.

Glue the edges of the two bills together with the exception of about 1/3 of the top left corner edge.

This opening at the top of the bill creates an opening into a pocket between the two bills.

When you begin, show this gimmicked bill on both sides using your thumb and index finger to hold the opening shut. Now holding the bill rightside up, roll the bill into a tube. Use your finger to enlarge the opening at the top so that the tube begins to look more like a funnel (wide at the top and narrow at the bottom).

Take a dime and place the dime into the opening of the special pocket. It will look like you are actually placing it into the funnel itself. Tip the opening of the funnel away from the audience slightly so that they can't see where the dime is actually going.

Wave your hand over the bill and show that the coin has disappeared by slowly unrolling the bill. Put the bill into your pocket next to an unprepared bill.

If they ask to see the bill, withdraw the normal bill to have them examine it.

ADDITIONAL IDEAS might include performing the routine in slow motion for them FIRST. In the slow motion part, don't ever leave the dime in the funnel but rather bring it back out with your hand and put it in your pocket. They will laugh because it will be so obvious! The next time actually do the routine at regular speed as written. They will wonder why they never saw your hand go to your pocket. Explain that "the hand is indeed quicker than the eye!"

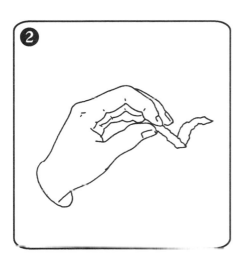

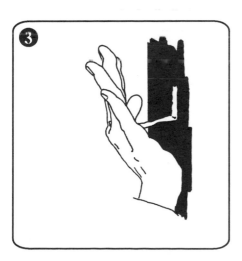

In the midst of the seminar, the trainer notices that a huge piece has been gouged out of the wallpaper in the room. The wallpaper has actually peeled back from a spot and hangs loosely from the wall!

The trainer simply walks over to the spot and covers the gouge with her hand. Upon removing her hand, the wallpaper is as good as new!

Before your seminar group arrives, find a piece of newspaper with no printing on either side (usually one of the margins works fine).

Tear a strip about three inches long by 1/2" wide. Make sure that you tear both sides of this strip so that all of the edges are jagged edges.

Fold the strip in half and apply moisture to one half of the strip, sticking that half to the wallpaper. The loose half of the strip needs to be at the bottom of the strip you just stuck to the wallpaper.

Now curl this loose half of the strip downwards, and it will begin to look like the wallpaper has pulled loose from the wall.

When ready to demonstrate this illustration, show the group the tear and press your hand against the strip with your fingers spread a little so that you are able to grip a little of the loose piece between your fingers.

Close your fingers and withdraw your hand, taking the strip with you. Take a few steps back and while all eyes are on the wallpaper, drop the strip into your pocket!

Tricks for Trainers 77

Any item small enough to hold in your hand can be made to disappear!

Stand with your right side towards the audience and place the item you wish to have disappear into your right hand.

Take a pen and tap the back of your right hand two times. Before you tap your hand each time, raise the pen up high enough to touch your left ear.

As you raise the pen for the third tap, slip the pen into the collar of your shirt. Practice so that you can do this with as little hesitation as possible so that you don't break the rhythm established by your previous taps.

As you go to tap your hand the third time, act surprised that somehow the pen has disappeared! Give a brief moment for the effect to register on the audience and then turn your body so that the left side is facing the audience. Point to the pen with your left hand pulling it out of your shirt collar and showing how you put it into the collar.

While you are explaining how the pen disappeared, casually drop the small item from your right hand in to a coat or pants pocket on your right side. However, keep your hand closed as through it still contained the object.

Turn around again so that your right side again faces the audience and turn your closed right hand so that the back of that hand now faces the floor.

Again tap the hand three times with the pen. On the third tap, let the hand open to show that the item has disappeared.

Use a small item symbolic of something you want to disappear as a result of your presentation and lead in by simply stating that "If I were a magician, I suppose that I could simply make it disappear. . . "

"However, since I'm not a magician it will take more work than that! That's exactly what we're going to be examining in our presentation today!"

Tricks for Trainers   79

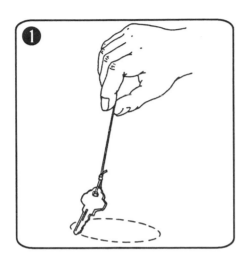

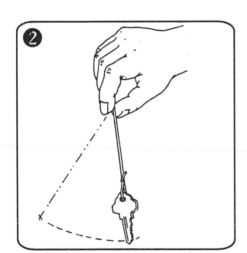

Each person in the seminar constructs a pendulum from a piece of string and a key. They hold the pendulum with the key hanging loosely at the bottom. As the trainer makes suggestions, the pendulums are made to swing in a circle first, stop, and then swing in a straight line. The suggestibility of the human mind is illustrated in a manner that won't soon be forgotten!

The illustration shows how each person holds their pendulum between their thumb and index finger.

Simply begin talking about the keys swinging in a circle and they will! Talk about the keys stopping and they will! Talk about the keys swinging in a straight line and they will!

Most of the people will be unaware of the small muscle movements of their hand making it all work.

If you want a little sound effect, have the people suspend their keys inside of drinking glasses. The keys will eventually begin hitting the side of the glasses, creating quite an auditory experience!

Each seminar member holds his fingertips apart. However, when the seminar leader begins suggesting that the fingertips are coming together, they do! All over the room!

Have everyone in your seminar clasp their hands together while extending their two forefingers. There should be a gap of about one inch between the forefingers.

Mention to the group that they could probably hold their index fingers like that all day. Except that you are about to make a suggestion to them about how tired their fingers are getting.

Talk to the group about how tired their fingers are feeling and how good it would feel to just let those two fingertips touch. Continue with this direction for about fifteen seconds and most fingertips in the room will have begun to move closer together!

    Tricks for Trainers   83

One of the smallest seminar members stands against a wall with arm outstretched — pushing against the wall. Other class members line up behind her — putting their hands on the shoulders of the person in front of them. Upon command, they push — attempting to push the front person into the wall. It can't be done!

See the diagram to appreciate how this looks. As long as the person against the wall can cope with the person directly behind her (you'll want to be sure that she can), the rest of the people's work will come to naught.

Although it looks impressive, it is quite an ineffective way to accomplish the job since each person absorbs the energy of the person behind them and inertia is the result of all the effort.

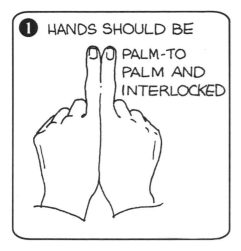

① HANDS SHOULD BE PALM-TO PALM AND INTERLOCKED

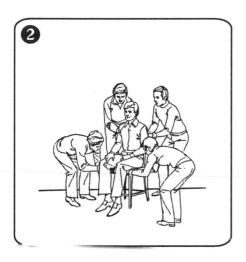

②

③

This demonstration illustrates the importance of attitude in success. As one member of the audience sits on a chair, four others stand around him. Using only two fingers each, these four people try to lift the person sitting in the chair with no success.

Now, the trainer begins to speak about the possibility of such an experiment. After the positive input from the trainer, the four lift the person in the chair effortlessly. The individual looks like he has indeed achieved weightlessness!

The person who is going to float must sit relaxed in a straight back chair with his knees together and feet flat on the floor.

Each of the others hold their hands with fingers interlocked and index fingers extended. One person places his fingers in one armpit while another puts his fingertips in the opposite armpit.

The other two each take a knee and put their fingers underneath the knees.

The first time you let them try to lift the man, don't attempt to coordinate their efforts. They will pull from all directions to no avail.

The second time explain to them how easy it really is and encourage them to try it again as you count to three.

As you reach the number three, they will exert their efforts in coordinated manner, and the man will rise off the chair.

This dramatic demonstration has four men pitting their strength against one woman in an unbelievable demonstration of working smarter versus working harder!

Ask the four men to arrange themselves in two pairs facing each other. You then pick up two broomsticks and a long length of rope. Each pair must grasp the end of the broomstick horizontally at arms' length as in the illustration.

Have the men stand about two to three feet apart and tie one end of the rope to one end of one of the broomsticks. Now wind the rope zig-zag fashion around the broomsticks five or six times — making sure that the ropes don't cross each other at any point.

Now have a woman come and take the free end of the rope while the men do their best to keep the broomsticks apart.

As the woman pulls the men will be drawn together! The more times you wind the rope, the easier you make it for the woman.

Section Three

This section has magic tricks designed to be first performed by the trainer and then taught to the members of the training class to help emphasize a point through hands-on involvement.

A pencil and dollar bill are both borrowed from the audience. With a tongue in cheek lecture about the danger of paper cuts, then the trainer sets up a demonstration.

A person holds the pencil between her hand while the trainer strikes it with the folded edge of the dollar bill.

Suddenly, the pencil breaks into two pieces upon being struck by the paper. It's sudden and traumatic! The explanation lends itself to helping an understanding of risk taking and the fears that keep us from achieving our potential.

Have one person hold the pencil (use a nearly new pencil for best results — the longer the better) very tightly by the ends in a horizontal position.

She must keep the pencil steady and must be holding it firmly.

Fold the dollar bill in half lengthwise and hold by one end between your thumb and the middle knuckle of your index finger. Raise the bill and lower it to the edge of the pencil several times.

Then bring the bill down forcefully after you have secretly extended your forefinger along the length of the bill.

Hit the pencil in its middle with the middle knuckle of your index finger. Determine to follow through without hesitation and the pencil will break as though it were made of putty.

The only problem you might have would be in the grip of the volunteer on the pencil. Make sure she holds it firmly!

After explaining how the trick works, encourage volunteers to come and try it. Many lessons can be taught from the reactions of the group!

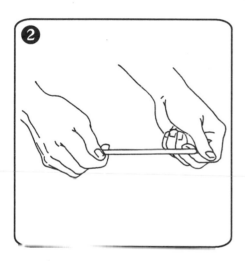

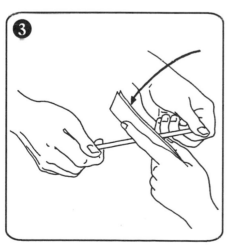

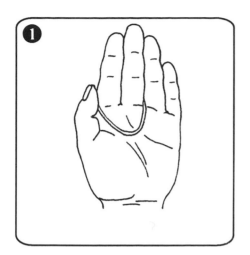

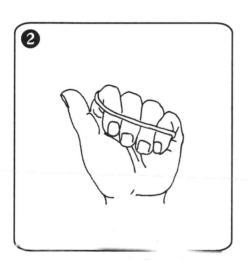

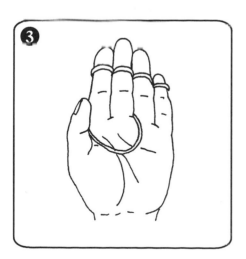

If the story is told, a trained rubber band performs tricks by jumping in a most unexpected manner!

Place a rubber band around the first and second fingers of one of your hands. Hold the hand up with its back towards the audience, the fingers extending upward. The rubber band should be loose enough for a small part of it to hang down on the palm side (figure 1).

With the other hand, snap the palm side of the rubber band once or twice. When you are about to snap it again, pull the band out and curl the fingers towards the palm so that they are all within the rubber band as in figure 2.

Your hand should now be held in a fist with the back of your hand facing upward. Don't show the audience that the band is now on your fingers. Only show them the front part of your fist and it will appear as though the rubber band is still around just two fingers.

Now straighten your fingers. Don't spread your fingers as you open your hand. Don't pull any of your fingers out of the rubber band. Instead, simply push the rubber band off your fingers by opening your hand.

The rubber band will leave your first two fingers and be wrapped around your third and fourth fingers.

You can make this even more mysterious by using another rubber band. After having the first rubber band in place at the base of your first and second finger, take the second rubber band and loop it around the tips of the fingers so that it ties the fingers together as in figure 3. Now it certainly appears as if it would be impossible for the rubber band to jump like it did in the first part of this routine. However, try it just like before and you will find that the first rubber band can jump just like before!

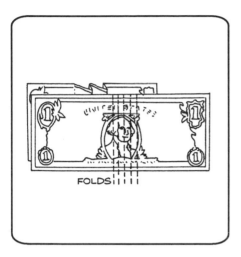

Everyone removes a dollar bill from their pocket. With only a little explanation from the trainer, each audience member suddenly looks at George Washington and sees him smiling broadly! By looking at the picture another way he suddenly looks mad! It's all a matter of perspective!

Try this yourself with a dollar bill.

Fold the bill in half so that a crease is made right down the middle of George Washington's mouth. The green side should be folded to the outside.

Now open the bill and make two more creases, one at each corner of George's mouth. These two creases should be folded in the opposite direction of the first crease so that George's mouth looks like it has two mountain peaks at the corners with a valley running down the middle.

Pull on the ends of the bill to flatten it a little and watch George's mouth as you move the bottom up towards your face and then down away from your face. It will appear as though George Washington moves from smiling to frowning and back again!

It's fun as the whole room sees the same thing happening with each of their bills!

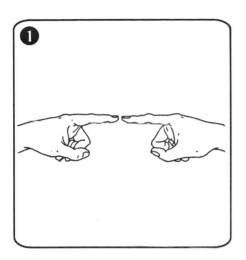

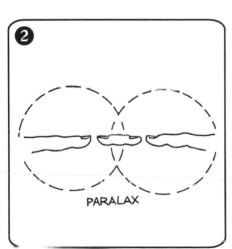

PARALAX

"HOT DOG"

The trainer helps each person make what appears to be a small hot dog float in the air right in front of their eyes!

The most unusual aspect of this demonstration is the fact that only the person floating the hot dog can see it!

It's a great demonstration for illustrating individual perspectives!

Have group members hold their outstretched index fingers of each hand horizontally with their fingertips touching.

Have them hold their fingers a few inches in front of the bridge of their nose. The other fingers are bent back into their palm. Have each person focus their eyes on some common point in the front of the room.

Now while focusing on the object in the front of the room, have them slowly raise their fingertips in front of their eyes — pulling their fingertips apart slightly.

It will appear as though a small hot dog is floating between the fingertips!

However, keep focused on the image in front of the room. Don't focus on the hot dog or it will disappear!

Any straight object (pen, knife, ruler, etc.) can be made to float! This is great for teaching how the details we don't see often cause us to be misled!

Rub a pencil on your sleeve as though trying to build up a high level of static electricity.

Then lay the pencil across your left palm, holding it in place with your left thumb.

Standing with your right side towards the audience, shake the left hand — holding the pencil with your left thumb.

Continue shaking your left hand by grabbing your left wrist with your right hand. The back of the right hand is toward the audience.

Turn so that your left side is now towards the audience and the back of your left hand is facing the audience.

During that turn extend your right index finger into the palm of your left hand to hold the pencil.

Stop shaking your left hand and slowly extend your left thumb so that the group can see that the pencil is sticking to your hand.

As you swing back around so that your right side again faces the audience, pull back in your index finger and hold the pencil again with your thumb.

As you teach this to the group, there is room for many applications!

   Tricks for Trainers   101

The spectator has a completely free choice of three cards shown to her. In spite of this, the trainer has successfully predicted her choice beyond a shadow of a doubt!

Take any three playing cards and place them into an envelope. On the back of one of the cards, make a large X with a permanent marker.

On the face of the envelope write the name of one of the other cards (not having the X).

Write the third card's name on a piece of paper and place it into the envelope with the three cards.

Begin the routine by simply saying that you have made a prediction of something that is about to happen. Remove the three cards from the envelope. Practice so that you don't show the prediction on the envelope or the prediction on the card in the envelope or the X on the back of one of the cards.

Now you will simply finish the routine in one of three ways. You can't lose. You will be right no matter which card the spectator chooses. If she chooses one card, you will show that it is the only card with the X on the back. You have predicted correctly.

If she chooses another, you will turn over the envelope and show the prediction matches the card the spectator chose.

If she chooses yet the third card, you will remove the prediction from the envelope showing that there is no other card in the envelope. Again you have been correct!

This routine really amazes even though it might seem simple to you as you read it!

Afterwards, let your seminar participants brainstorm on how it might be done. It's a great exercise in creative problem solving!

   Tricks for Trainers   103

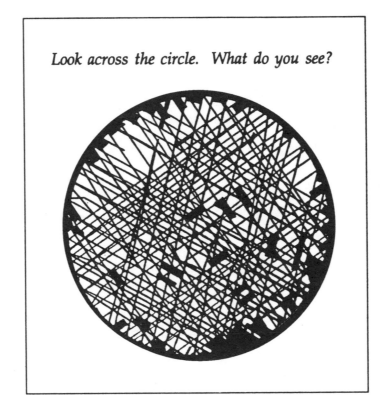

Look across the circle. What do you see?

What looks like simply a modern art design with no discernable purpose, suddenly becomes an actual message when viewed from the proper perspective.

This comes complete with a guide for putting any message you want into the design to really make your message have impact with a handout that will be kept!

The design you see in the circle is actually a message. In order to see it, hold the book right side up and bring the bottom of the circle up towards your face. You will be viewing across the circle in order to see the message.

The letters are very tall and run from the top of the circle to the bottom. Closing one eye sometimes helps people first see the words. Holding the book at arms length is also sometimes helpful. The first words you should see are the words:

"IF YOU LIKE FUN"

Don't get discouraged if it takes awhile. In a group, you will have some who get it right away and then will turn and help others see the message.

After seeing the first words in the message, turn the bottom of the book clockwise and more words will come into view!

The entire message hidden in the circle is:

IF YOU LIKE FUN AND LEARNING TOO CREATIVE TRAINING IS FOR YOU!

You will find the entire alphabet in these special letters on page 106. By building one of these circles yourself, you will have a personalized handout that will definitely be kept by group members to show their friends!

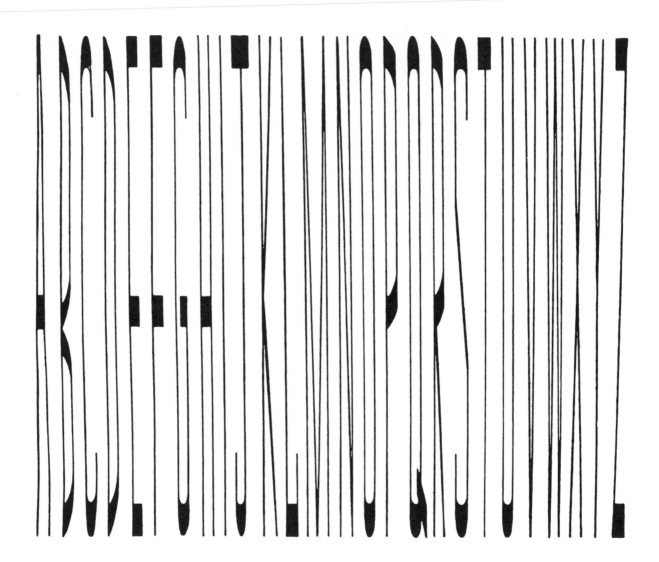

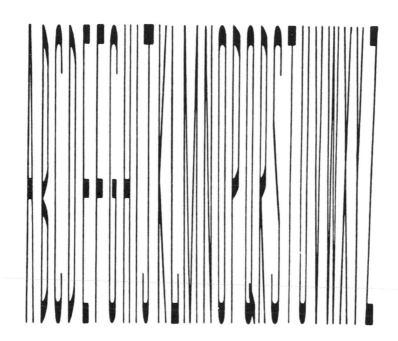

The trainer carefully (and with apparent skill) balances a cup on the EDGE of a plate! It totters at first and won't balance but finally precariously stays on top of the plate.

The explanation always brings laughter and helps the class understand how easily we can be fooled by situations we don't carefully examine.

Pick up the plate (china will work fine but you might want to practice with plastic) holding it at about the two o'clock position if the back of the plate is viewed as the face of the clock.

Your thumb should be at the back of the plate with the rest of your fingers at the front towards the audience.

Take a cup and try to balance it at the twelve o'clock position on the top edge of the plate. Several times you should let it teeter and fall catching it with your free hand.

When ready to get it balanced, extend your thumb behind the plate so that it can touch the bottom of the cup and give it the secret help it needs.

Slowly, turn your hand around so that the audience can see how easy it is to miss an important detail as you analyze a situation.

Tricks for Trainers   109

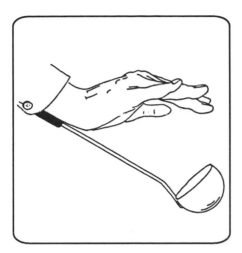

The trainer stands with what appears to be a silver ball in his hand. The ball gently floats off the hand and rises up to meet the other waiting hand.

The audience is mesmerized by what they're seeing until they realize that the silver ball is the bowl of a soup ladle, the handle of which was stuck up the long shirt sleeve of the trainer!

Watch the viewing angles of your audience on this one. However, usually if the people are seated directly in front of the trainer, there will be no problem.

The hand of the stainless steel soup ladle is inserted up one of your long shirt sleeves with the bowl of the ladle resting in the palm of your hand. The rounded bottom of the bowl faces out towards the audience and looks like a silver ball.

Tell your group that you've been working on a little magic and want to show them one of your latest attempts.

Place your other hand over the bowl and reverse your hands so that the arm with the handle is now on top. Slowly move your top hand up and the ball will appear to be floating up with your hand!

Suddenly, show the audience exactly what they've been watching by pulling the handle out of your sleeve!

In order to get into the secret position in front of a group, have the ladle in a large shopping bag and insert both arms to grab the ball — inserting the handle under the cover of the paper sack.

Tricks for Trainers   111

The trainer complains about a pain in her shoulder. She wonders if maybe she didn't put it out of joint in her rather rigorous exercise program. She asks an audience member to gently push on the shoulder for her.

As someone does just that, there is suddenly a loud cracking sound that causes all in the room to jump!

When the trainer explains, she has a natural lead in to the subjects of perspective, cause and effect, assumptions, or creative problem solving.

Prior to your training group's arrival, take one of those hard plastic hotel type glasses and put it in your armpit under your coat or sweater.

As the person pushes on your shoulder, bring your arm in towards the side of your body and the cup will crack with a loud noise. No doubt the person doing the pushing will react with a very sudden response! Just what you wanted!

Tricks for Trainers   113

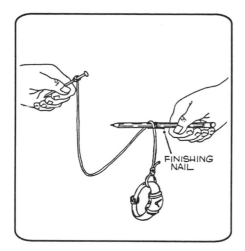

The trainer borrows a watch and ties it to a string — hanging the string over a pencil. The trainer wants to know how long the class believes it will take the watch to drop and hit the floor. Unbelievable as it may seem, the outcome of letting go of the string is completely unexpected — much to the relief of the person lending the watch.

This is a great demonstration for illustrating the fear of failure!

You will need a piece of string approximately four or five feet long and a pencil. Tie a finishing nail (2" long) to one end of the pencil.

When you're ready to present this demonstration, borrow an expensive watch and tie it to the end of the string opposite the nail.

Have the volunteer hold the nail end of the string while you drape the watch over the pencil in your hand.

Ask the group how long they believe it will take for the watch to hit the ground. If you really want to give the owner of the watch a mild heart attack, you could put a bowl of water on the floor underneath the watch.

On the count of three, have the volunteer let the nail go.

The group will be amazed to see the watch never hit the floor as the nail wraps the string around the pencil in your hand!

Who would have thought it!

Tricks for Trainers   115

Section Four

This section contains TEN audience-tested early bird exercises to use as people gather in the training room.

Each one is in the form of an easily copied transparency master for use with your overhead projector.

Each exercise has been designed to emphasize a different component necessary for maximizing creative thinking!

It is possible to
drink out of this
can WITHOUT
puncturing it,
opening it, or
destroying it
in any way!

HOW?

Preparation: Make a transparency from the master on the opposite page — place it on your overhead projector. Also put an unopened can of pop on your overhead projector positioning it so that class members can easily see it.

Solution: Take the can of pop and turn it upside down — pouring a little water into the recessed bottom of the can. Then drink the water. You have just drunk "out of the can without puncturing it, opening it or destroying it in anyway!"

Application: As with all of these early bird exercises, it is good to take some time to analyze just why solving this problem was so difficult.

Many times it has to do with an incomplete or inaccurate definition of the problem!

S E C U R A

The letters above can be arranged to spell a common English word!

HOW?

Preparation: Use the master on the opposite page to make a transparency — place it on your overhead projector.

Solution: The word is "SAUCER."

Application: This seems so easy but is really quite difficult. Once a person pronounces the word SECURA even in his mind, the mind has trouble finding its way to the correct solution.

Their are seven misstakes in this pargraph! If you can find all seven misstakes, you are smarter then the average person you're age!

Preparation:	Make a transparency from the master on the opposite page — place it on your overhead projector.
Solution:	The seven mistakes are as follows:

1) THEIR should be spelled THERE;

2) MISSTAKES should be spelled MISTAKES;

3) PARGRAPH should be spelled PARAGRAPH;

4) MISSTAKES is again misspelled;

5) THEN should be spelled THAN;

6) YOU'RE should be spelled YOUR; and

7) There are only six mistakes in this paragraph. That is the seventh mistake!

Application:	Many times people will begin to find mistakes that aren't mistakes just to have seven mistakes!

 Tricks for Trainers 123

It can be proven
that this piece
of wood is out
of Noah's Ark!

HOW?

Preparation: Make a transparency from the master on the opposite page — place it on your overhead projector. Also, place a piece of wood on the overhead. The more unusual looking the piece of wood the better!

Solution: It is obvious from looking at the piece of wood that it is not IN Noah's Ark! Therefore, the wood must be OUT OF Noah's Ark! It's a matter of semantics!

Application: Communication is quite important!

PNLLEEEESSSSS

The letters above can be arranged to spell a common English word!

HOW?

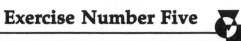
Preparation: Make a transparency from the opposite page — place the transparency on the overhead projector.

Solution: SLEEPLESSNESS

Application: Many just won't try this one because it seems formidable. Others will give up after one or two attempts. Backing up and trying again is necessary for maximizing creative thinking.

Tricks for Trainers 127

In just a moment a volunteer's head will be pushed right through this bracelet!

HOW?

Preparation: Make a transparency from the master on the opposite page — place it on your overhead projector.

Also have a bracelet laying on the over-head projector so that the outline is projected onto the screen. You can even draw an arrow to the bracelet so that people make the connection.

Solution: After obtaining a volunteer, insert your hand through the bracelet and push the volunteer's head with that hand.

You have just pushed a volunteer's head "right through the bracelet!"

Application: We often make things more difficult than they really are and overlook the simple solution.

Often the simple solution is the best solution.

Tricks for Trainers   129

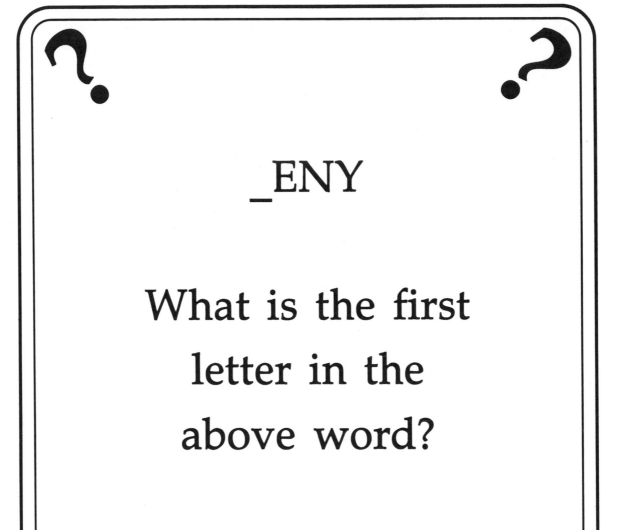

_ENY

What is the first letter in the above word?

Preparation:	Make a transparency from the master on the opposite page — place it on your overhead projector.
Solution:	DENY
Application:	Most people will attempt to solve this by moving through the alphabet, inserting different letters in the front of the word.

Unfortunately, by the time they get to the letter D, they are already in a rut and pronounce DENY like DENNY — missing the solution to the problem.

We can get into mental ruts very quickly!

I saw an oak creeping
on the ground
I saw a snake
swallowing up a whale
I saw a blue sea full
of pop
I saw a cup as big as
the moon and higher
I saw the sun red even
at midnight
I saw the person who
saw these sights!

How can it be proven?

Preparation: Make a transparency from the master on the opposite page — place it on your overhead projector.

Solution: To prove the paragraph true, punctuate it!

I saw an oak. Creeping on the ground,
I saw a snake. Swallowing up a whale,
I saw a blue sea. Full of pop,
I saw a cup. As big as the moon and higher,
I saw the sun red. Even at midnight,
I saw the person who saw these sights!
Haven't we all seen these things?

Application: Don't limit yourself by making up rules. No one said you couldn't punctuate the paragraph. Don't make false assumptions.

  Tricks for Trainers 133

There are at
least two ways
to cut the string
so that the
cup will remain
suspended
from the string!

HOW?

Preparation: Make a transparency from the master on the opposite page — place it on your overhead projector.

Hang a cup (mug) from the ceiling by a piece of string tied to the handle of the cup.

Solution: You may simply cut a little piece off the loose end of the string extending from the knot tied around the handle of the mug. This won't affect the cup's suspension.

Or... you can tie a loop in the string and then cut the loop. The cup will remain suspended.

Application: There is usually more than one correct answer to any question we face.

Often times, we look for only THE RIGHT ANSWER. We can miss THE BEST ANSWER.

    Tricks for Trainers   135

Many things which appear to be impossible ...aren't!!

Try building one of these yourself!

Preparation: Make a transparency from the master on the opposite page — place it on your overhead projector.

Also, build the unusual display example given.

Taking a glass, a half dollar and two forks, balance the half dollar on the very edge of the glass using the two forks to shift the center of gravity so that it does balance.

Put the two forks across the coin, letting their upper tines hold them in place as in the picture.

Then rest the edge of the coin farthest from the tines on the lip of the glass, moving the fork handles outward or inward gently until you have a balance.

Set this display on your overhead projector so others can see it as they enter the room.

Have glasses, half dollars, and forks available for others to use in building their own.

Application: First appearances can be deceiving. Many will fail in attempting to build this display, but like in life, persistence will reward many.

Tricks for Trainers 137

Section Five

This section contains ELEVEN of the greatest brain-teasers (brain busters, braintwisters) of all time!

They are great for putting a break in a seminar and for illustrating many different emphases about how our thought processes work.

They really help to maintain a creative and interactive environment!

Preparation:	Have a volunteer from the group stand on a chair.
Presentation:	You challenge the volunteer with the words:
	"Before I count to three, you'll be off that chair and on the floor! I won't touch you. No one in the class will touch you. It's purely mental!"
Solution:	Say "One," then "Two," and then continue speaking to the class forgetting the person on the chair. They will indeed be off the chair before you count to three, since you won't count to three until they do step down off the chair.
Application:	A good way to use braintwisters like this is to issue the challenge and then give the group time to try and figure your approach.
	Often times, they will invent even better strategies. At the least they will have participated in a non-threatening exercise in creative problem solving — complete with all the essential ingredients necessary for solving more complex problems.

   Tricks for Trainers   141

Preparation:	Take the nickel and the penny and place them in one of your hands — closing that hand into a fist.
Presentation:	You state the situation to the group using these words:
	"I'm holding in my hand two American coins. When added together, their value totals six cents. However here's the most remarkable fact one of them is NOT a nickel."
	Really emphasize the word "not" as you state the facts.
Solution:	You are holding a nickel and a penny, and the penny is the coin that isn't the nickel!
Application:	This one is excellent to use in explaining any subject involving communication skills.
	You can go back and analyze your presentation of this braintwister. Show how tone of voice, inflection, and word choice misled your audience.

Preparation: Have a book of paper matches handy and one book for each person at the seminar if you want them to think it through with you.

Presentation: Mention how you've noticed that one side of a paper match is usually a little different shade than the other one.

Toss a match in the air once or twice — letting it land on a table to show how no one can control which side of the match will land face up.

However, now tell the group that you have become skillful enough to toss the match high in the air (above your head) and land on the table so that it always lands on its edge!

Have them brainstorm to try and discover how to accomplish this impossible feat.

Solution: Bend your paper match in half and toss it in the air. It will land on its edge.

Application: This is a great braintwister for analyzing the process of creative brainstorming!

Tricks for Trainers   145

It Figures!

$1000

40

1000

30

1000

20

1000

10

Preparation:	Use the transparency master on the opposite page to make a transparency.
Presentation:	When ready to present the braintwister, cover all of the digits with a piece of paper except the one at the top of the column (1000).
	Pull your paper down the column only one digit at a time, having your audience add the digits out loud before moving to the next digit in the column.
Solution:	If you show them only one digit at a time and have them add in their heads as they go along, the majority of people will arrive at 5000 for a final answer.
	The correct answer is 4100. You can test it with a calculator.
Application:	By taking one number at a time, there is a rhythm that develops and the rhythm falsely leads the viewers to a wrong conclusion.

Tricks for Trainers

Preparation: Use the transparency master on the opposite page to make a transparency.

Presentation: When ready to present this braintwister, turn on your overhead projector and go to a person in your audience and casually ask them to read what's on the overhead projector.

Then go to another one or two and ask them to read the overhead.

Solution: Most in your audience will have read the message as "Rabbit in The Hat!"

When you stop and show them that the word "THE" appears twice in the slogan, they usually can't believe it!

Application: Here our mind is tricked by a seemingly common expression further defined by the art work.

We assume we see it clearly and become careless — causing the extra word to slip by our consciousness.

EASY MONEY!

Deposit $2,500.

Withdraw	Balance
$1,000.	$1,500.
750.	750.
450.	300.
300.	0.
$2,500.	$2,550.

Do this ten times= $500.

Preparation:	Use the transparency master on the opposite page to make a transparency.
Presentation:	Place the transparency on the overhead projector and lecture for a brief moment on the perfect way to make $500 per day!
Solution:	Even after explaining the figures, the reason why this works is very difficult to define.
Application:	This opens a group to admitting that there are things they don't understand.
	This attitude is essential to good learning!

Preparation: Have a full can of pop and a book of matches on a table for the group to see.

If you want them to experiment with this challenge, have a can of pop and a book of matches available for each person.

Presentation: You present the challenge to the group using the following words:

"The challenge is simple. Get the book of matches completely under the bottom of the can of pop without anyone touching the can of pop."

Solution: Place the book of matches under the table so that it is also directly under the can of pop!

Application: This is a braintwister that illustrates well how we limit ourselves with our own self-made restrictions!

 Tricks for Trainers 153

Preparation: Have an old light bulb (or several) handy for this excellent demonstration.

Presentation: The challenge is to drop the light bulb on a cement floor from a height of at least five feet and not have the light bulb break.

Nothing can be wrapped around the light bulb or put on the floor to cushion the fall.

Solution: Drop the light bulb like a hot air balloon so that it lands directly on the bottom of the brass portion at the bottom of the bulb.

Unbelievable as it may seem, the light bulb may bounce around, but it will not break.

The base will absorb the shock of the drop.

Application: If you don't have a cement floor, you can stand on a chair and drop it onto an undraped table.

Or you can bring in a square of plywood and place it on the floor.

This braintwister will have people working so hard to figure out how to cushion the fall of the bulb but never stopping to experiment to find out if the bulb would actually break if dropped just as it is!

We often spend so much time thinking when a little time doing would be more efficient.

Preparation: Stretch a rope across the front of the room and have a person hold each end.

Thread a bracelet (one that is solid and doesn't have an opening) onto the rope.

Presentation: You present the challenge with the following words:

"In just a moment, I will pull this bracelet right off the rope without either person letting go of her end."

Solution: Dramatically, you grab the bracelet and pull it up so that it no longer is touching the rope.

You have indeed pulled the bracelet "right off the rope" just as you said you would.

Now, tell them that there is still at least one other solution and let them go to work on it.

You can slide the bracelet to one end of the rope and pull it right off the rope over the hand of one of your volunteers! This also would qualify as pulling the bracelet "right off the rope."

Application: A discussion of assumptions and mental visualizations could logically follow this braintwister, since it was assumptions and the consequential false mental picture that led them astray.

The multiple solution aspect to this braintwister also helps the group understand that there is often more than one right answer.

Tricks for Trainers 157

Preparation: Hang two strings from the ceiling in the front of the room so that while holding one string in your hand and stretching you still are about two feet short from being able to reach the other one.

Presentation: The challenge is to grab one string in each hand with no help from anyone else. You are allowed only to use such items as might be in your pocket or purse.

Solution: Tie a key to one of the strings as a weight — swinging that string like a pendulum so that it swings far enough over so you can grab it with one hand while holding the other string with your other hand.

Application: This one is a good one to begin with at the start of the day and not bring to a solution until later in the day.

The challenge creates a good climate in the room for creative interaction.

The process of solving this problem is very much the process needed to solve any problem we face.

Tricks for Trainers 159

Preparation: Make some time to read the following story.

Presentation: Read the following story to the group.

A tabloid carried the following story.

"Wife Kills Husband with Newspaper!"

A husband and wife sat in their living room both reading the evening paper. The husband dozed off and began to dream.

He was a man who lived in France — convicted of a crime when the guillotine was still in use. The day of his execution came. As he walked up the platform to the guillotine, the bright blade gleamed in the sunlight. He knelt by the guillotine and inserted his head in the fateful opening. His neck was secured in place. Out of the corner of his eye, he watched as the executioner reached to grab the cord that would release the blade. As the executioner pulled the cord, he could now hear the blade descending towards his neck.

At exactly this moment, the man's wife leaned over to awaken him and tapped him on the back of his neck with the paper she had been reading. The man slumped forward in his chair — dead. The coroner's report indicated that he had died of a massive heart attack — no doubt due to intense fear!

How do you know that this story could not be true.

Solution: If it were true there is no way that we would ever have known the story of his dream.

Application: What made this so difficult? In this situation, most people get caught up with the details of the story (i.e. "Did the French use guillotines? Did they execute during daylight? etc.) that they miss the main incongruity of the story.

Someone else has called it something about "missing the forest for the trees."

Dave Arch

Since 1982, Dave Arch has pioneered the use of magic in his motivational programs and training seminars.

In those years, magic has proven itself an effective communication tool for groups as diverse as hospital CEO's to sales representatives to banking administrators.

Combining a ten year background in personal and family counseling with a professional expertise in magic, Dave travels from his home in Omaha, Nebraska, to present his unique presentations before some 25,000 people each year in both corporate and conference settings.

Whether he's using a power saw to saw an audience volunteer in half or attempting to escape from a regulation straitjacket, his audiences long remember both the excellent content and the entertaining audience involvement that have become the trademarks of his successful presentations.

Robert has developed and implemented training programs for business, industry, government and the professions since 1969. As president of Resources for Organizations, Inc. Creative Training Techniques International, Inc., and The Resources Group, Inc., Bob leads sessions over 150 days per year covering topics of leadership, attitudes, motivation, communication, decision-making, problem-solving, personal and organizational effectiveness, conflict management, team building and managerial productivity. More than 50,000 trainers have attended the Creative Training Techniques® workshop. As a consultant Bob has worked with such organizations as Pfizer, Upjohn, Caesars Boardwalk Regency, Exhibitor Magazine, Hallmark Cards Inc. and IBM.

Over the years Bob has contributed to magazines like "Training," "The Personnel Administrator" and "The Self Development Journal." He is editor of the "Creative Training Techniques Newsletter" and is author of "The Creative Training Techniques Handbook," "Developing, Marketing and Promoting Successful Seminars and Workshops" and "Improving Managerial Productivity."

The Creative Training Techniques Companies

Resources for Organizations, Inc.
Creative Training Techniques, Int'l. Inc.

The creation of these companies has resulted in working together for one goal: to help clients achieve exceptional results with the application of innovative and creative training and development technologies.

Resources for Organizations, Inc.(ROI) was the first of the companies which make up the successful Creative Training Techniques Companies. ROI is committed to providing resource materials which enhance the results of your training. The resources Bob Pike and his master trainers use during their seminars are available through the Resources for Organizations, Inc. (ROI) catalog. Many of ROI's products, like Tricks for Trainers, can turn training sessions into fun, stimulating, and memorable experiences. While other materials, which are rich in content, are full of practical and useful "how to" techniques. Whether it is integrating new interactive learning activities or utilizing training props, trainers at any level can enhance their sessions with these simple yet powerful tools.

In addition to this variety of training materials, activities, books, and props, ROI is the exclusive source for the audio cassette tape program featuring Bob Pike leading the popular two-day Creative Training Techniques™ workshop.

Creative Training Techniques International, Inc. (CTTI) conducts seminars and in house programs to build trainers competencies with instructor led, participant-centered techniques. As a result of these programs, Bob and his trainers are able to unleash the learning potential of adults. Whatever your level of experience, by attending these seminars you will increase audience involvement, improve the clarity and organization of your presentation and ultimately get better results.

Whether your need is for effective training products, practical and dynamic seminars, or useful pre-packaged programs, the Creative Training Techniques Companies can assist you in achieving your training and organizational aspirations. Please call (612) 829-1954 for further information and literature.

    Tricks for Trainers   165

The Resources Group, Inc. (TRGI) focuses the application of Creative Training Techniques programs and products which develop a company's most important asset - its people. The Resources Group, Inc. (TRGI) was formed to develop and conduct training programs utilizing those processes that address the "Human Side of Enterprise." All of TRGI's programs use the Creative Training Techniques' process of high energy and high involvement, with a focus on the application of knowledge and skills to achieve results.

Whether your need is for effective training products, practical and dynamic seminars, or useful pre-packaged programs, the Creative Training Techniques Companies can assist you in achieving your training and organizational aspirations. Please call (612) 829-1954 for further information and literature.